All the Papas

A True Love Story
for Fathers and
Their Children

Written and Illustrated by
Carol Gandee Shough

Summerhouse Press
Columbia, South Carolina

In loving memory of my dad, Roy and my father-in-law, Wren

the two best grandpapas my children could ever have

Published in Columbia, South Carolina

Copyright 1999 by Carol Gandee Shough

P.O. Box 1492 Columbia, South Carolina 29202
(803) 779-0870
(803) 779-9336 fax

Printed in Hong Kong through PrintNet

FIRST EDITION

Library of Congress Cataloging-in-Publication Data
Shough, Carol Gandee.
    All the papas : a true love story for fathers and their children / written and illustrated by Carol Gandee Shough. -- 1st ed.
        p.   cm.
    Cover title.
    Summary: Based on genealogical records going back to the eighteenth century, this work describes significant events in the lives of fathers and their sons or daughter.
    ISBN 1-887714-36-7
    [1. Fathers and sons--Fiction. 2. Fathers and daughters--Fiction.] I. Title.
    PZ7.S55883Am   1999
    [E]--dc21   99-12234
                                                        CIP

The illustrations were created in oil pastel and colored pencil.

In the middle of the vast Pacific, on a tiny speck of land, on an island paradise filled with wondrous sights and sounds, a perfectly ordinary miracle took place. A child was born.

A young Papa held his precious bundle and made a promise then and there. "I will protect. I will provide. As best I can, I will."

In the middle of the lagoon, the baby beach it's called, on a surfboard painted red, Aitana and her Papa Rick splashed the warm, saltwater foam. The playground made of sand and shells sparkled with love and life.

"Aitana, hold on tight. Your Papa's here. All right!"
Then Papa Rick paddled out with babe perched upon his board. They peered through aqua depths for fish and felt the power of the tides.

4

5

As Aitana kicked and splashed with glee
and learned to trust and float, her Papa Rick
placed his hand beneath her head and spoke.
"I just can't stand it. You are so cute,
you water baby you. Hold your breath and
plunge right in. I am so proud of you."

On that warm, Hawaiian beach
Rick's Papa smiled and watched
those two and thought of water,
wind and waves.
And he remembered when. . .

. . .in the middle of a man-made lake, in a sturdy boat with sails, he and Rick, a small boy then, raced before the wind. Towards the leeward mark the Texas sky was dark with storm clouds moving in.

9

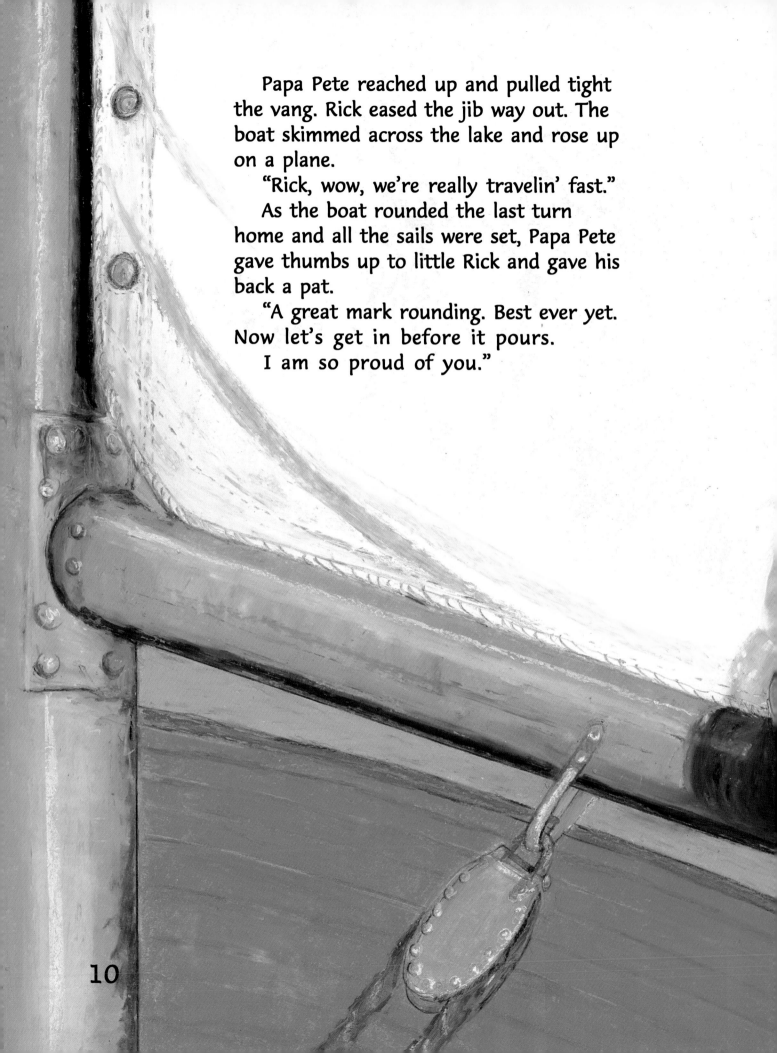

Papa Pete reached up and pulled tight the vang. Rick eased the jib way out. The boat skimmed across the lake and rose up on a plane.

"Rick, wow, we're really travelin' fast."

As the boat rounded the last turn home and all the sails were set, Papa Pete gave thumbs up to little Rick and gave his back a pat.

"A great mark rounding. Best ever yet. Now let's get in before it pours.

I am so proud of you."

11

On that rocky, Texan shore
Pete's Papa filled his pipe and
watched them race.
     And he remembered when . . .

12

. . . in the middle of a northern lake, in a
canoe well worn, he and Pete, a small boy then,
sat so straight and tall. In tandem strokes
and downward pulls, their paddles plunged into
the lake. On either side two swirling rings were
left behind in wake. Up and foward, dip and pull.
The steady pace kept on.

14

"Pete, look over there."

Papa Wren pointed to the camp. Pete dragged his paddle on the left and positioned it just so. As the canoe turned slightly right and glided towards the bank, his Papa Wren turned and winked.

"Your first time steering is on the mark. A perfect landing! I declare.
I am so proud of you."

On a dusty road called
Rebert's Pike, Wren's Papa read
a postcard from Maine that
pictured lakes and camps and
drying racks of fish.
    And he remembered when . . .

16

. . . in the middle of a winding creek that flowed behind the barn, he and Wren, a small boy then, pulled at their fishing poles. Papa Frank put his finger near his lips and pointed down the stream.

"Wren, the fish are feeding now. See the ripples beside the bank."

The fishing line drifted to that spot. A rainbow trout bit hard. Wren jerked the line; the hook was set. The fish was his at last.

Then Papa Frank looked at the sun and said, "It's quittin' time, I bet." He packed the creel with green, wet leaves and the freshly netted trout.

As the two paraded up the hill, Papa Frank bent down near Wren and looked him in the eye.

"A three-pound trout, I reckon so!
I am so proud of you."

19

On a farmhouse porch just down the Pike, Frank's Papa sat and rocked and hoped they'd caught some fish.

And he remembered when . . .

. . . in the middle of a quiet pond, on a water-logged tree trunk, Frank, a small boy then, sat alone and cried. His eyes filled up with tears. Papa William beckoned from the bank.

"Frank, your Mama's home from church just now. The preacher said the prayers. We need you here with us. Please come."

Papa William had buried four children within that week. The deadly pestilence had disappeared, but left behind deep grief. He thought, "I have three more to raise. I will protect. I will provide. As best I can, I will."

He held small Frank, his eldest now, and choked back the sobs inside.

"We must get back. The parlor's full of folks who came to pay respects. You helped us all, my strong, young son.

I am so proud of you."

At the gravesite around the bend, William's Papa bowed his head and closed his eyes.
And he remembered when . . .

24

   . . . in the middle of an Ohio field, just partially
cleared of trees, he and William, a small boy then,
poked along beside the oxen team.
   "Look there, Papa. I spy a pheasant in between
the rows," William's young, joyful voice piped up.
   Papa Isaac grinned and wiped away the sweat.
He turned and briefly caught a glimpse. The
pheasant disappeared between the stacks of hay.
   Just then the oxen shook their ponderous heads
and strained beneath the yoke. Papa Isaac gave a
shout,
   "William, watch that stump. We've got it almost
yanked plum out."

When shadows reached the berry patch, the grueling work was done.

"Will, let's get the dogs and hunting guns and check up on the traps. Let's catch that bird you spied about an hour past. I think you have the eagle's eye. I am so proud of you."

Far away that very day, in a
Pennsylvania town, Isaac's Papa
poked the fire and roasted
gamebirds that he just caught.
And he remembered when . . .

28

. . . in the middle of the virgin woods, among the tall pine stand, he and Isaac, a small boy then, stood their ground and held their bows in hand. An arrow flew, but missed the mark. The deer bounded across the glen. Papa Joseph touched Isaac's arm and spoke with heart felt pride.

"Isaac, son, the hunter's prize will soon be yours. Ne'er mind the last missed shot. I am so proud of you."

On a peaceful, puffy cloud
by heaven's pearly gates, all the
Papas gazed earthwards.

And each remembered when . . .

. . . in the middle of a restless sea,
a Papa and his small child pulled the
teeming nets.

. . . in the middle of a village green a
Papa and his small child pounded hot,
molten bronze.

. . . in the middle of a prairie, parched
brown beneath the sun, a Papa and his
small child ploughed the crusty earth.

. . . in the middle of a sea of sand a Papa
and his small child packed the desert
caravan.

. . . in the middle of an ancient plain a Papa and his small child panted hard as all pursued the mighty, woolly mammoth herd.

. . . in the middle of a high plateau a Papa and his small child provided poems and songs to all inside the cave.

. . . in the middle of a primeval isle a Papa and his small child prayed to gods, protectors of their clan.

All the Papas coaxed and taught and passed along their trades. All the Papas spoke the words, "I am so proud of you."

Genealogy of All the Papas

Aitana Elizabeth was born in the late 1990s in Hawaii.

Her Papa **Richard James** was born in the middle 1960s and grew up in Central Texas near the Highland Lakes. He married Sharon Hildalgo-Prahl. He works in the tourist industry on Maui.

His Papa **Peter Baldwin Shough** was born in the late 1930s and raised in Ohio. He married Carol Elizabeth Gandee. He worked in marketing and sales and is now retired.

His Papa **Wilbert Wren Shough** was born in 1907 and raised in Ohio. He married Sarah Thelma Baldwin. He taught biology at the high school and college levels.

His Papa **Frank Shough** was born in 1875 and raised in Ohio. He married Nellie Evans. He was a farmer, teamster and blacksmith.

His Papa **William Shough** was born in Pennsylvania in 1829 and raised in Ohio. He married Charity Jane Green. Four of their children died of diphtheria within a two week span during a summer epidemic. He started out as a hired hand and later owned his own farm.

His Papa **Isaac Shough** was born in 1805 in Pennsylvania. He married Mary Carle and migrated to Ohio with his young family. He was a pioneer settler.

His Papa **Joseph Shough** was born in Pennsylvania in 1761. He married Catherine Schlisler and had twelve children. He was a musketmaker.

His Papa was born in Germany and immigrated with his Papa in the early 1700s.

The birds that inhabit the pages of *All the Papas* represent the geographic area where each Papa lived.

Hawaii—Bird is the parrot. Flower is the bird of Paradise. Fish are parrot fish and angelfish.

Texas—Bird is the road-runner, depicted in the Austin Yacht Club burgee.

Maine—Bird is the loon, excellent swimmers and feeders of fish in lakes of the North Woods.

Ohio—Bird is the cardinal, the Ohio State Bird, The mourning dove, named for its low, mournful sound, and the pheasant, plentiful in farmlands and grassy woodland edges.

Pennsylvania—Bird is the wild turkey, common in the pine-oak forests of colonial America.

Heaven—Bird is the dove, symbol of peace.

7/09 $

199 $